READING ABOUT

My Home

By Jim Pipe

Aladdin/Watts
London • Sydney

In the city

2

Hi, I'm Rosa and I live in the city.
My home is in a tall block of flats.

Our flat is on the tenth floor, so I
take the lift to get home.

Taking
the lift

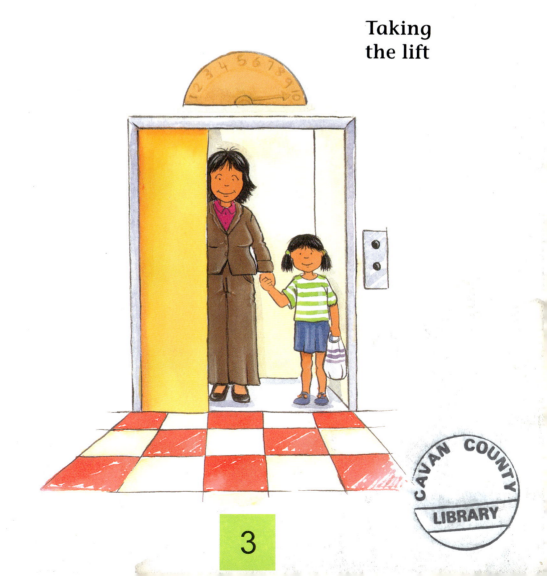

3

There are flats above and below us. Our flat has two bedrooms.

My sister Beth and I share a room. We sleep in bunk beds.

Bunk beds

At night I can see the city lights from the top bunk.

The city is a great place to be!

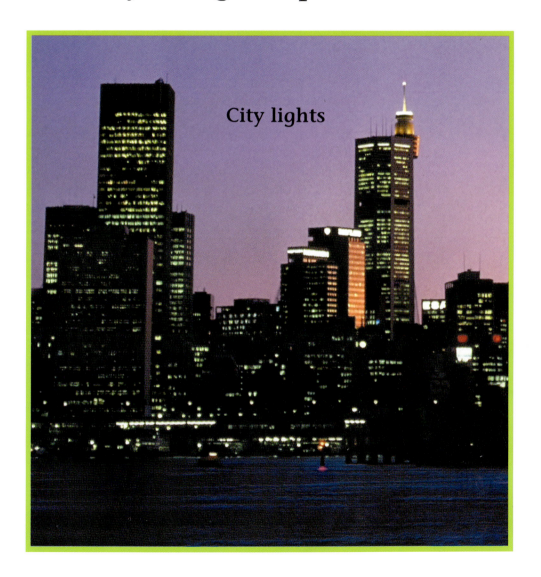

City lights

City people rush here and there.
I like to watch them from the bus.

Sometimes cars get in a jam and
drivers honk their horns.

Bus

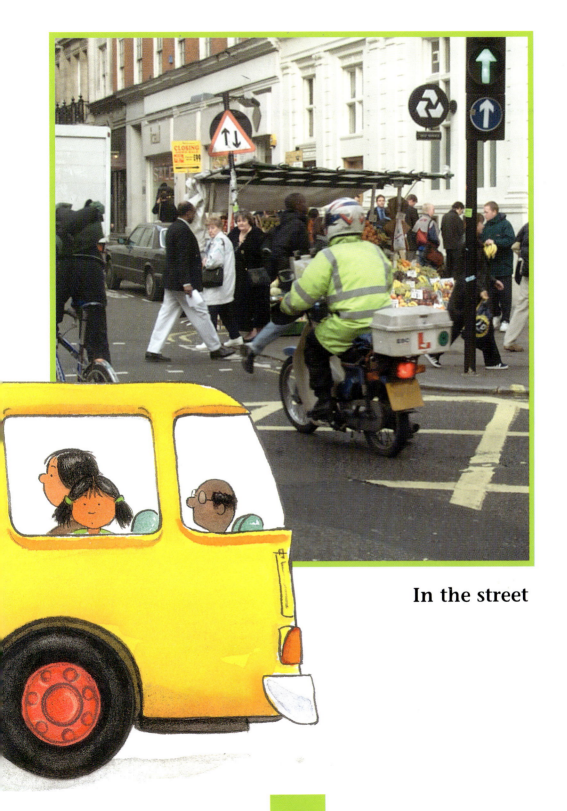

In the street

7

Hi, I'm Jack and I live in the country. It is very quiet here.

From my window I can watch the cows and sheep in the fields.

Window

I can hear birds singing in the trees at the end of my garden.

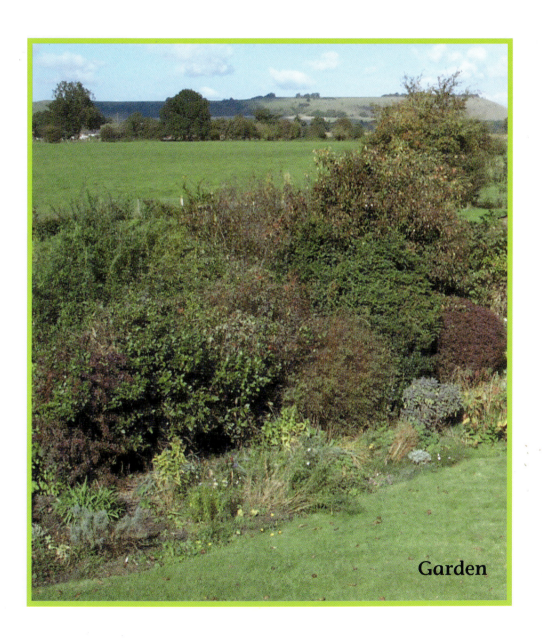

Garden

Our home has three bedrooms.
We also have a workshop. We
are making a birdhouse.

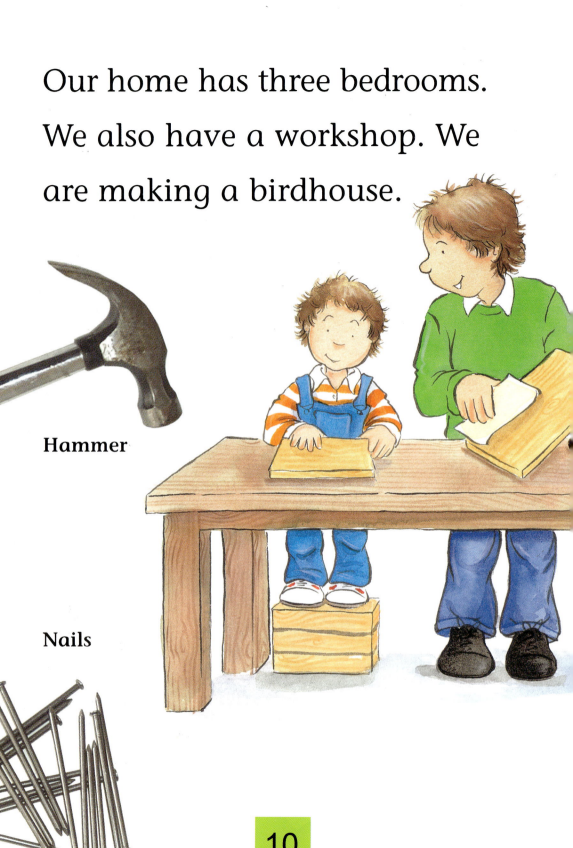

Hammer

Nails

Dad cuts the wood with a saw. I rub the wood smooth with sandpaper.

Then Dad knocks in the nails with a hammer.

Saw

Sandpaper

Our neighbours are the Jacksons. They live across a field.

On their farm they have cows, chickens and pigs.

Farm

Sometimes Mr Jackson lets me sit on his tractor.

The country is a great place to be!

Tractor

Hi, I'm Andy. I live in the suburbs.

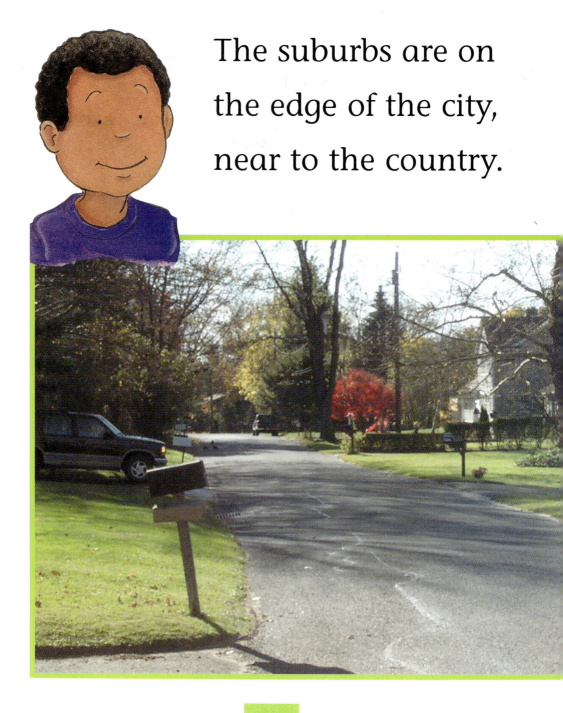

The suburbs are on the edge of the city, near to the country.

From my window, I can see
the other houses in my road.

They have trees and bushes
in their gardens.

The suburbs

Our house has three floors. My room is at the top, in the attic.

Attic room

I have to climb a lot of stairs to get to my room.

Sliding down

But I do not have to walk down.

If I am careful, I can slide down!

My friends Joe and Billy live next door.

We love swinging on the rope in Billy's garden.

On the rope

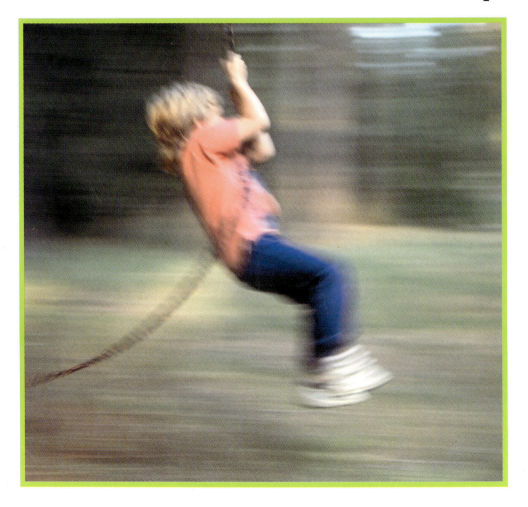

Often we ride our bicycles up
and down the pavement.

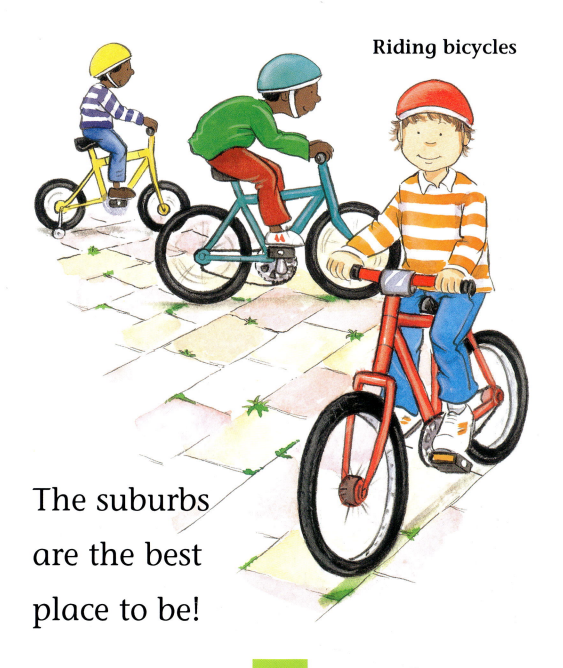

Riding bicycles

The suburbs
are the best
place to be!

Rosa, Jack and Andy all think
their home is a great place
to be.

Where do you live?

What do you like
about your home?

Here are some words and phrases from the book.

Swing on a rope

Ride on a bus

Sleep in bunk beds

In the country

Sit on a tractor

Slide down

Live in the city

Lift

Ride bicycles

Can you use these words to write your own story?

Did you see these in the book?

Poster

Scooter

Clouds

Carpet

© Aladdin Books Ltd 2001
All rights reserved
Designed and produced by
Aladdin Books Ltd
28 Percy Street
London W1T 2BZ
Literacy Consultant
Phil Whitehead
Printed in U.A.E.

First published in
Great Britain in 2001 by
Franklin Watts
96 Leonard Street
London EC2A 4XD

A catalogue record for this
book is available from the
British Library.

ISBN 0 7496 4846 5

Illustrator
Mary Lonsdale - SGA
Picture Credits
All photos by Select
Pictures except 2, 5,
23 tr - Corbis; 18, 22tl -
Digital Stock.